A New True Book

ENERGY

By Illa Podendorf

*This "true book" was prepared
under the direction of
Illa Podendorf,
formerly with the Laboratory School,
University of Chicago*

CHILDRENS PRESS, CHICAGO

PHOTO CREDITS

Tony Freeman—2, 29, 37 (left)

Candee & Associates—4, 20, 37 (middle)

Lynn M. Stone—6 (2 photos), 8 (left), 12, 27, 33 (2 photos), 39, 41, (right)

James M. Mejuto—Cover, 7, 8 (right), 14 (bottom), 25, 26 (left), 30 (bottom), 37 (right)

Inland Steel Co—26 (right)

James P. Rowan—9, 13 (right), 28, 41 (left)

Art Thoma—30 (middle)

Bill Thomas—10, 11, 21, 30 (top), 34, 35

Jerry Hennen—16, 22, 42, 45

M. Cole—24

David Glazewski—13 (left), 17

Tom Winter—19

Joseph A. Di Chello, Jr.—14 (top)

American Bowling Congress—36

COVER—Deep sea oil rig

Library of Congress Cataloging in Publication Data

Podendorf, Illa.
  Energy.

  (A New true book)
  Rev. ed. of: The true book of energy. 1963.
  Summary: An introduction to various sources
of energy, including wind, water, electricity,
magnets, heat, and sunlight.
    1. Power resources—Juvenile literature.
2. Force and energy—Juvenile literature.
[1. Power resources. 2. Force and energy]
I. Title.
TJ163.23.P6   621.042   81-12309
ISBN 0-516-01625-3   AACR2

TABLE OF CONTENTS

OUR ENERGY

In winter we can go sledding. We sled on a hill.

We climb up. We slide down.

We use much energy when we climb the hill. But we use less energy when we slide down.

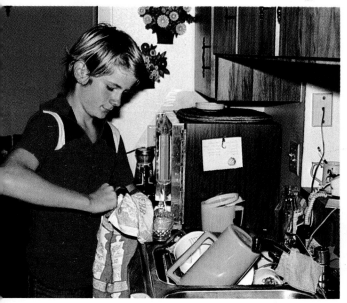

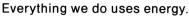
Everything we do uses energy.

We use energy to work. Making a garden is hard work. Taking care of the lawn is hard work. Washing dishes is hard work.

We need a great deal
of energy to do work.
We use our energy to
work and play.

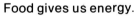
Food gives us energy.

Good food gives us
energy. We could not work
or play without good food.
Rest helps us store up
our energy. Then we can
work and play again.

8

Polar bears playing at the zoo

Animals use energy
when they play. They get
energy from the food they
eat.

Animals use energy
when they work. Elephants
get energy from plants
they eat.

People have learned to make and use other kinds of energy. They use the wind. They use fuels like coal and oil. They make electricity.

Each kind of energy can make other kinds of energy.

Coal-fueled power plant on the Ohio River

WIND ENERGY

Wind is moving air. It can be used to do work.

Wind turns our pinwheels when we hold them up.

Wind turns windmills. The turning windmill can pump water.

    Wind makes a sailboat
go.

    Wind has much energy.
It can be very strong.
Sometimes it blows trees
down.

WATER ENERGY

Fast-running water has energy. It rolls stones over and over each other.

Water sometimes washes away dirt. It may take plants with it, too.

Mabry Mill in Virginia

The force of running water is sometimes strong. It can be used to turn a waterwheel.

A big waterwheel may turn other wheels. The other wheels may be used to do work for us. They can grind corn in a mill.

Waterwheels can do other work. They can help us make electricity.

ELECTRICAL ENERGY

Electricity is made by machines. These machines are called generators. Parts turn inside the generator. The different parts turning around each other give us electricity.

This experimental turbine wind generator was built in Clayton, New Mexico, by General Electric and the United States Department of Energy.

Many different kinds of energy make a generator work. Sometimes water energy is used. The water turns wheels. These wheels turn the generator parts.

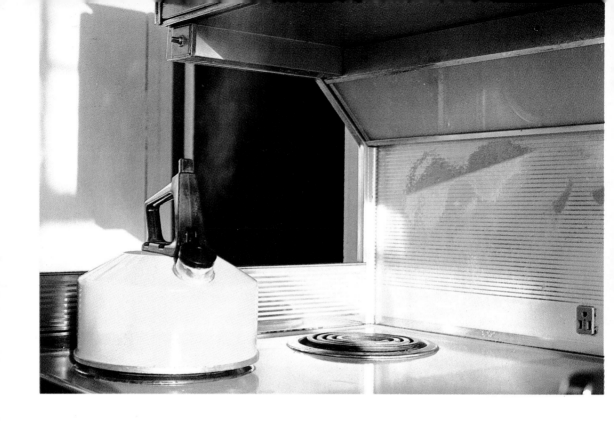

Sometimes heat energy
is used. A fuel is burned.
Water boils from the heat.
Boiling water makes steam.
The force of the steam
turns generator parts.

Nuclear power plants use atomic energy.

Another kind of energy used is atomic energy. Atoms are split up. This makes a great deal of energy. This energy runs a generator.

Men working on an electric power line

Electricity is made at places called power plants. When the electricity is made, it is sent out. It runs through thick wires called cables. The cables go to places where electricity is used. Homes, schools, offices, and factories all use electricity.

Electrical energy is used to do many kinds of work. It runs washing machines. It turns fans. It saws down trees. It makes light bulbs light up.

Can you think of other things it does?

New York City at night

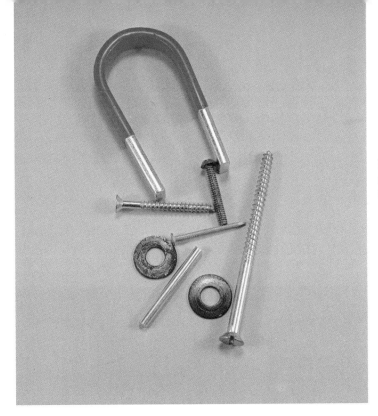

Magnets attract things made of iron or steel.

MAGNETIC ENERGY

All magnets have magnetic energy in them. Magnets can be made to do work for us.

A compass has a magnet in it. The magnet always shows us where north is. An electromagnet is very strong. It can be used to pick up heavy pieces of metal.

Above: Compass
Right: Electromagnet

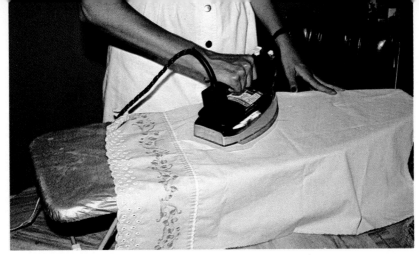

Electricity
is used
to heat
this iron.

HEAT ENERGY

We get heat energy in different ways.

Electricity can make heat energy. Electricity gives an iron its heat energy. Electricity can be used to heat buildings. Electricity can give a stove its heat energy to cook foods.

We also make heat
energy by burning fuels. A
campfire gives off heat
energy. Wood is its fuel.
Stoves can burn wood or
gas for heat energy.

Heat energy can cook
our food. But heat energy
from burning fuels can do
other kinds of work, too.

Heat energy changes water to steam. Steam takes up more room than water. Steam pushes with great force. The force of steam can be used to make an engine go.

An old steam engine, Western Coal & Coke Engine #1

Above: Delta Queen
Left: Aircraft in flight
Below: Cars use gasoline
as fuel.

A steamboat uses the force of steam. Steam makes its wheels turn in the water.

Cars and planes burn fuels. The fuels they burn make their engines work. The engines give them the power to move.

We get heat energy in many ways. Much heat energy also comes from the sun.

SUNLIGHT

The sun's energy is very important. We get energy from the foods we eat. But the foods' energy comes from the sun.

Sunlight helps plants grow. Energy from the sun is stored in plants.

Sunlight helps corn and tomatoes grow in gardens.

Much of our food comes from plants. We eat many plants. In this way we get energy from the sun.

Some of our food comes from animals. Many of these animals eat plants. The animals get energy from the plants. We get energy from these animals.

Meat we eat and milk we drink come from animals that have eaten plants.

People have found ways to store the sun's energy, too. They can make solar cells. Solar cells are put in sunlight. The cells change the sunlight into heat energy or electrical energy.

Solar energy can heat homes. It can be used to run machines.

By directing the sun's rays with a magnifying glass this artist is burning a sign into wood.

SOME OTHER KINDS OF ENERGY

This ball shows energy. It rolls down the lane. It pushes over the pins.

The energy of the ball comes from its motion.

Skateboarding, roller skating, and bike riding are examples of energy in motion.

All of these things will have energy when they are set in motion.

Putting some kinds of things together makes energy. The energy can do work. This is chemical energy.

Take a teaspoon of baking soda. Add two tablespoons of vinegar to it in a glass. Many bubbles are made. The bubbles fill up the glass. They are strong enough to push most of the air out of the glass.

This is an example of chemical energy at work.

There are chemicals in a
flashlight battery. The
chemicals make electrical
energy. This lights the bulb
in the flashlight.

Light and sound are
kinds of energy, too. They
can also do work.

A laser can make a light beam. This light beam is very strong. It can cut through metal and other things.

Sounds make the air shake. Sounds can be changed to radio waves. Radio waves can be sent out. The waves carry sound to our TVs and radios.

Sounds can also be changed to electrical energy. Electricity carries the sound on our telephones.

First stage engine of the Saturn V rocket

People use many kinds of energy to travel in space. Rockets burn fuel. Some spacecraft use solar cells for energy.

MANY KINDS OF ENERGY

We use our energy when we work and play. We get energy from the food we eat.

We use energy from the wind and from running water. We use energy from magnets and from fuels we burn.

One kind of energy we can make is electrical energy. It is made by generators.

Another kind of energy is heat energy. We can get heat energy in many ways.

We call some kinds of energy mechanical energy. Still others are chemical energy.

We use energy to send sound to telephones, radios, and TVs.

Energy can be used to travel on land, on water, in the air, and in space.

   Sunlight is a very
important kind of energy.
   With no energy, the
Earth would be cold, dark,
and quiet. We need energy
to live.

WORDS YOU SHOULD KNOW

atom—the smallest bit of an element that can exist alone

bank—the sloping ground at the edge of a river or lake

chemical—something formed when two or more substances act upon each other

depend(dih • PEND)—to rely on

diesel(DEE • zill)—an engine that burns oil

electrical—something heated, made, run, or moved by electricity

energy(EN • er • gee)—power to do work

engine—a machine using the energy of steam, gasoline, or wood

fuel(FYOOL)—anything that is burned to give off heat or energy

furnish(FER • nish)—give

generator(GEN • er • a • ter)—a machine that makes electricity

grind(GRYND)—to turn into small pieces by pounding or crushing

magnet—an object made of iron, steel, or other material that can be made to attract iron.

motion(MO • shun)—movement

solar—of or related to the sun

INDEX

About the author

Born and raised in western Iowa, Illa Podendorf has had experience teaching science at both elementary and high school levels. For many years she served as head of the Science Department, Laboratory School, University of Chicago and is currently consultant on the series of True Books and author of many of them. A pioneer in creative teaching, she has been especially successful in working with the gifted child.